SOPHIE
GRIGSON

FROM SOPHIE'S TABLE

PENGUIN BOOKS

PENGUIN BOOKS

Published by the Penguin Group. Penguin Books Ltd, 27 Wrights Lane, London
w8 5tz, England. Penguin Books USA Inc., 375 Hudson Street, New York,
New York 10014, USA. Penguin Books Australia Ltd, Ringwood, Victoria, Australia.
Penguin Books Canada Ltd, 10 Alcorn Avenue, Toronto, Ontario, Canada m4v 3b2.
Penguin Books (NZ) Ltd, 182 – 190 Wairau Road, Auckland 10, New Zealand · Penguin
Books Ltd, Registered Offices: Harmondsworth, Middlesex, England · These
extracts are from *Sophie's Table* by Sophie Grigson, published by Michael Joseph
1990. Published in Penguin Books 1992. This edition published 1996. Copyright ©
Sophie Grigson 1990. All rights reserved · The moral right of the author has been
asserted · Typeset by Rowland Phototypesetting Ltd, Bury St Edmunds, Suffolk.
Printed in England by Clays Ltd, St Ives plc · Except in the United States of America,
this book is sold subject to the condition that it shall not, by way of trade or otherwise,
be lent, re-sold, hired out, or otherwise circulated without the publisher's prior
consent in any form of binding or cover other than that in which it is published and
without a similar condition including this condition being imposed on the subsequent
purchaser · 10 9 8 7 6 5 4 3

CONTENTS

Starters and Egg Dishes

Pear and Stilton Soup   3

Smoked Haddock and Onion Soup   4

Carrot and Rice Timbales   5

Shrimp Beignets   6

Leek and Carrot Kuku with Stilton   7

Apple and Goat's-cheese Omelette   8

Huevos a la Flamenca   9

Deep-fried Radicchio with Goat's Cheese   11

Vegetables

Hot Beetroot and Apple with Sour Cream   15

Smothered Broccoli   16

Sesame Roast Jerusalem Artichokes   17

Bamia   18

Mushroom and Aubergine Moussaka with
Gremolata   19

Onion Tart   21

Hot Potato and Pepper Salad   22

Raw Tomato Sauce   23

Main Courses

Pasta with Anchovy Sauce and Poached Eggs 27

American Crabcakes 28

Red Mullet and Red Pepper Tart 29

Moroccan Paprika Chicken 31

Chicken with Soy Sauce 32

Chicken and Tarragon Patties 33

Savoy Cabbage and Ham au Gratin 34

Pork Chops with Onion and Pear Marmelade 36

Pork Medallions with Mushrooms and Sorrel Sauce 37

Spiced Lamb Sausages with Tzatziki 38

Puddings

Hunza Apricots with Yoghurt 43

Crème Normande 44

Blood Oranges in Rosemary Syrup 45

New York Cheesecake 46

Blackberries in Filo Pastry 48

Frozen Chocolate Mocha Mousse 49

Cranberry Tart 50

Marmalade Ice-cream with Walnut Sauce 52

Starters and Egg Dishes

PEAR AND STILTON SOUP

Pears and Stilton, apples and Cheddar, simple companions but
real soul mates. Here is that marvellous balance of salt and sweet,
the flavour of the cheese highlighting that of the fruit and vice
versa. Hard to beat.

This soup is lighter and less cloying than the classic Stilton
soup, which I love but find terribly rich. To add a contrasting
crunch to the soup, serve with tiny baked croûtons.

SERVES 4

1 onion, chopped
15 g (½ oz) butter
4 medium-sized ripe pears, cored, quartered and chopped
¾ litre (1½ pt) chicken stock
salt and pepper
125 g (4 oz) Stilton
juice of ½–1 lemon
fresh chives, chopped

In a large pan, cook the onion gently in the butter, without browning. Add the pears and the stock, and a little salt and pepper.
Simmer until the pears are very tender. Pass through the fine blade
of a *mouli-légumes*, or liquidize and sieve. Return to the pan and
reheat, without boiling. Add the Stilton and stir until dissolved.
Sharpen with lemon juice to taste, and adjust the seasoning.
Sprinkle the chives over the top and serve.

If you make this soup in advance, reheat without boiling.

SMOKED HADDOCK AND ONION SOUP

A smoked haddock soup may sound a touch perverse, but don't let yourself be put off by that. There's just enough fish to give a mild smokiness. Try your very best to find undyed smoked haddock.

SERVES 4

250 g (8 oz) smoked haddock, skinned and chopped
½ kg (1 lb) onions, chopped
2 cloves of garlic
1 sprig of thyme
45 g (1½ oz) butter
¾ litre (1½ pt) milk
salt and pepper

Melt the butter in a pan large enough to take all the ingredients. Add the onion, whole garlic cloves and thyme. Stir and cover. Cook over a very gentle heat until the onions are meltingly tender – this should take at least 30 minutes, and is even better if cooked really gently for 45 minutes. Stir occasionally.

Add the haddock to the onions, and cook for a further 5 minutes. Pour in the milk, and add a little salt and plenty of freshly ground pepper. Bring to the boil and simmer for 10 minutes. Pass through a *mouli-légumes*, or liquidize and sieve. The soup should be fairly thick, but if necessary add a little extra milk. Taste and adjust the seasoning. Reheat and serve with toast or croûtons.

CARROT AND RICE TIMBALES

These are simple to concoct, and can be either a first course or a vegetable accompaniment to a main course.

There's no reason at all why you shouldn't adapt the recipe to other vegetable purées (such as celeriac, pea, broad bean) with considerable success.

SERVES 6 as a first course or side-dish

½ kg (1 lb) carrots
2 eggs
1 tablespoon double cream
lemon juice
salt and pepper
1 sprig of tarragon
60 g (2 oz) rice
1 round lettuce

Slice and cook the carrots until tender. Drain well, and put in a blender with the eggs, double cream, a squeeze of lemon juice, salt, pepper and tarragon. Blend, and adjust the seasoning.

Cook the rice, drain and stir into the carrot mixture. Pluck 16 untorn leaves from the lettuce. Bring a large pan of water to the boil, drop the lettuce leaves in and bring back to the boil. Remove the leaves about 10 seconds later, rinse under the cold tap, and drain well.

Brush 6 small ramekins or dariole moulds with a little oil, and line with 1 or 2 lettuce leaves as necessary. Throw away any leftover leaves. Fill the moulds with carrot mixture, and flip any overhanging lettuce over the mixture. Cover each one with foil.

Stand the moulds in a roasting tray, filled to a depth of 2–3 cm (1 in) with water, and bake at 190C/375F/Gas 5 for 15 minutes. Lift out of the roasting tray and turn out on to individual dishes, or one large dish – in which case it's best to turn them out first on to a greased saucer, then slip on to the serving dish.

SHRIMP BEIGNETS

These crisp puffy little fritters are really out of this world, though I say so myself. I ate far more of them than was at all good for me when I was trying out the recipe, and in the end had to tip the remaining half of the batter out to prevent myself making just 1 or 2 more. Wasteful, I know, but I'd got to the stage where drastic measures did have to be taken, and fast.

SERVES 6

> *135 g (4½ oz) flour*
> *¼ teaspoon salt*
> *1 tablespoon oil*
> *1 egg, separated*
> *150 ml (¼ pt) lager*
> *350 g (12 oz) peeled shrimps*
> *¼ teaspoon cayenne pepper*
> *oil*
> *lemon wedges*

Sieve the flour with the salt into a mixing bowl. Make a well in the centre and add the oil, egg yolk and lager. Gradually beat in enough warm water to form a batter with a consistency of double cream – you'll probably need between 200–300 ml (⅓–¼ pt). Beat until smooth. Add the shrimps and cayenne pepper, and set aside until you are ready to use.

Fill a frying pan to a depth of 2–3 cm (1 in) with oil and heat, or use an electric deep fryer. While the oil is heating, whisk the egg white until stiff, then fold into the shrimp batter. Drop a dessertspoonful at a time into the hot oil, and fry until the top surface has just set and the underneath is lightly browned. Turn and brown the other side. Drain quickly on kitchen paper, and serve with the lemon wedges.

LEEK AND CARROT KUKU
WITH STILTON

A *kuku* is a Middle Eastern baked omelette, thick with vegetables. Like the Spanish *tortilla*, it can be eaten hot, warm (best of all) or cold, cut into wedges or squares. Stilton is about as un-Middle Eastern as you can get, I know, but the thin vein of cheese running through the centre adds a welcome hint of salt. The *kuku* is excellent as either a main course or part of a buffet, and it makes a perfect picnic dish.

SERVES 6–8 as a main course

9 eggs
3 leeks, trimmed
½ kg (1 lb) carrots, coarsely grated
4 spring onions, finely chopped
3 tablespoons fresh parsley, finely chopped
salt and pepper
butter
175 g (6 oz) Stilton, crumbled

Cut the leeks into 5 cm (2 in) lengths and shred. Drop into boiling water, bring back to the boil, then drain thoroughly. Cool. Break the eggs into a large bowl and beat well. Stir in the leeks, carrots, spring onions, parsley, salt and plenty of pepper.

Generously butter an oven-proof dish (a gratin dish, 5–8 cm (2–3 in) deep, 30 cm (12 in) in length is ideal) and spoon half the mixture into it. Sprinkle Stilton evenly over it, and cover with the remaining egg mixture. Cover with foil and bake at 160C/325F/ Gas 3 for 30 minutes. Remove the foil and bake for a further 15–20 minutes, until the eggs have set and the top is golden brown.

Cut into squares, and serve hot or warm from the dish, with buttered chicory and a baked sweet or plain potato. Or serve cold with salads.

APPLE AND GOAT'S-CHEESE OMELETTE

I find plain omelettes and even omelettes *aux fines herbes*, however perfectly made, boring and unsatisfying. I like bits and bobs in my omelettes, things that give that extra edge and interest. This recipe, speckled with goat's cheese, fulfils my concept of the ideal omelette.

SERVES 1

3 eggs
30–45 g (1–1½ oz) goat's cheese
1 sprig of thyme
1 small eating apple, peeled, cored and chopped
salt and pepper
15 g (½ oz) butter

Crumble the goat's cheese (or chop it finely if it's quite moist). Beat the eggs vigorously with the thyme, salt and pepper. Melt the butter and heat in a frying pan. When frothing, throw in the chopped apple. Sauté until beginning to brown. Distribute the cubes fairly evenly around the pan.

Give the eggs a final quick whisk and pour into the hot pan, tilting from side to side to ensure that the egg is evenly distributed. As the edges begin to set, scrape gently towards the centre, allowing the still liquid egg to fill the gaps. Continue to cook over a high heat, until the omelette is set underneath and *baveuse* on top – that is, thick and creamy, but not yet solid.

Scatter the crumbled goat's cheese in a wide band along a diagonal. Flip one side carefully over the cheese, then quickly flip the entire omelette out on to a warm plate, waiting patiently at the side. The omelette should be neatly folded in 3. Eat immediately.

HUEVOS A LA FLAMENCA

Huevos a la Flamenca, baked eggs with tomato, chorizo and green beans, is one of the standard dishes in southern Spanish tapas bars. I first tasted it in a seedy-looking place in Seville. It was love at first mouthful, in fact the beginning of my love affair with Spanish cooking.

Buy chorizo, the essential Spanish sausage, from good delicatessens. You should be offered the choice of mild or *piccante* – hot and spicy. Choose whichever suits your palate. Take the thicker, slicing sausage, 5 cm (2 in) or so in diameter, if available. Otherwise, slice the thinner chorizo into as many slices as seems reasonable and necessary. When asparagus is in season, try substituting it for the green beans.

SERVES 4 as a first course, 2 as a main course

4 eggs
125 g (4 oz) green beans
90 g (3 oz) shelled fresh peas, or thawed frozen peas
1 onion, chopped
2 cloves of garlic, chopped
scant tablespoon fresh parsley, chopped
2 tablespoons olive oil
125 g (4 oz) ham, roughly chopped
600 g (1¼ lb) tomatoes, skinned and chopped
125 g (4 oz) chorizo
salt
paprika

Top and tail the green beans, cut into 2½ cm (1 in) lengths and parboil for 5 minutes. If you use fresh peas, do the same with them.

Fry the onion, garlic and parsley in the olive oil until translucent. Stir in the ham, then add the tomatoes and fresh peas, if using. Simmer together for 10 minutes, stirring occasionally to make sure it does not catch. Add the green beans and the chorizo, whole, and continue to cook for 5 minutes. Stir in thawed frozen peas at this point, and simmer until the beans are just tender. Add a little extra water or stock if it becomes too thick and dry. Season with salt and paprika. Keep the sauce simmering very gently on the heat, and dredge out the piece of chorizo sausage. Cut into 4 thick slices.

Preheat the oven to 230C/450F/Gas 8. Take 4 oven-proof bowls, or 1 large one if you are serving it as a main course, and quickly divide the very hot sauce between them. Make a depression in the centre of each, and break the egg into it, letting the white flow across the surface. Cover the yolk with a slice of chorizo, and whip the bowls quickly into the oven. Bake for 8–12 minutes, until the white has barely set.

Serve quickly, with plenty of bread to mop up the juices.

DEEP-FRIED RADICCHIO WITH GOAT'S CHEESE

In winter months, when I want a quick, light lunch, I often toss a few radicchio leaves in French dressing, lay a slice of goat's cheese or crumbly Lancashire on top, and whip it under the grill. The heat turns the pretty maroon colour of the leaves to a less prepossessing brown, but it tastes wonderful.

Deep-fried radicchio, clasped in crisp layers of breadcrumbs, is even better, though it takes more time. Still, you can do most of the work in advance, leaving only the frying until the last minute.

SERVES 4

1 head of radicchio
seasoned flour
2 eggs, beaten
fine dry breadcrumbs
oil

Sauce:

60 g (2 oz) goat's cheese
150 ml (5 fl oz) soured cream or fromage frais
salt and pepper
1½ tablespoons fresh chives, finely chopped

To make the sauce, cut the rind off the goat's cheese and crumble. Beat or liquidize with the soured cream. Season to taste with pepper and a little salt, and stir in the chives.

Separate the leaves of the radicchio, wash and dry. Dust each leaf with flour, then dip in the beaten egg and coat thoroughly in breadcrumbs. The leaves can be prepared up to 4 hours in advance and kept in the fridge, covered loosely, until required.

Heat a large pan of oil to 190C/375F and fry the radicchio leaves until golden brown. Drain briefly on kitchen paper, and serve immediately with the sauce.

Vegetables

HOT BEETROOT AND APPLE WITH
SOUR CREAM

I don't like bought ready-cooked beetroot. Most are sozzled with vinegar, and rather unpleasant vinegar at that. Even those that aren't are still disappointingly dull.

A good vegetable deserves better treatment, and whatever your personal feelings about beetroot, it *is* a good vegetable. Indeed, I would even go so far as to say that it is up there among the top ranks, as long as it is freshly and plainly cooked.

SERVES 6 as a first course or side-dish

2 large cooked beetroot, peeled
2 eating apples
30g (1 oz) butter
salt and pepper
8 tablespoons soured cream, fromage frais or Greek
*   strained yoghurt*
2 tablespoons fresh chives or spring onion, chopped
6 slices of bread, crusts removed, or 30 g
*   (1 oz) breadcrumbs*

Cut the beetroot into 5 mm (¼ in) thick slices and halve. Quarter the apples and core, but do not peel. Slice the quarters thinly, so that they are about as thick as the beetroot. Arrange in a buttered gratin dish, or shallow oven-proof dish, in alternate overlapping bands. Season well and dot with the butter. Cover with foil, and bake at 200C/400F/Gas 6 for 20–30 minutes.

Meanwhile mix the cream with the chives. To serve as a first course, cut the bread into triangles and fry in butter or toast until golden. For a side-dish, fry or grill the breadcrumbs until golden brown and keep warm.

When the vegetables are ready, either tuck the triangles of bread around the edges, or sprinkle the crumbs evenly over the top. Spoon the soured cream down the centre of the dish. Serve while still hot.

SMOTHERED BROCCOLI

Instead of lightly cooking broccoli until it is just *al dente*, try it 'smothered' one day. This long, slow method of cooking vegetables intensifies their natural sweetness and transforms the flavour. Add a hint of garlic and the heat of red chilli, and the broccoli tastes sensational.

SERVES 4 as a first course or side-dish

½ kg (1 lb) broccoli
olive oil
1–2 dried red chillis, seeded and crumbled (optional)
2 cloves of garlic, sliced
coarse sea salt

Divide the thick stems of broccoli – more than 2 cm (¾ in) in diameter – in half or thirds down their length. Trim and rinse in cold water.

Cover the base of a heavy based skillet or frying pan (big enough to take the broccoli in a single close-fitting layer), with a generous layer of olive oil. Add the chillis and garlic. Cook over a medium heat until it sizzles. Add the broccoli, and coat in the oil. Reduce the heat to its lowest setting. Season with salt, and add a scant 150 ml (¼ pt) water. Cover tightly. Cook gently for 1 hour, turning the broccoli carefully 2 or 3 times.

The broccoli should be wonderfully tender, having absorbed most of the water. If it still seems very liquid, uncover and raise the heat to boil off some of the water. Serve hot or warm, with toast as a first course, or as a side-dish.

SESAME ROAST JERUSALEM ARTICHOKES

Pick out Jerusalem artichokes that are firm and as smooth as you can find. There's nothing wrong with the really knobbly ones; it's just that they are harder to peel in one piece, even after they are half cooked.

Eat them plainly boiled or steamed, or cooked, drained well and then sautéed in butter until thoroughly reheated and beginning to brown. For smarter occasions, or when you feel in need of a serious treat, try this recipe, coating them first in sesame seeds, then roasting them until the insides are meltingly tender and the outside is crisp and crunchy. The dish is good enough to eat as a first course on its own, or with the Sunday roast.

SERVES 4 as a first course or side-dish

½ kg (1 lb) Jerusalem artichokes
salt
5 tablespoons olive oil
2 cloves of garlic, chopped
2 dried red chillis, seeded and chopped

seasoned flour
1 egg, beaten
sesame seeds

Scrub the artichokes but do not peel. Parboil for 5 minutes in salted water. Drain and peel. While the artichokes are cooking, heat the oil with the garlic and chilli in a small pan set over a low flame for 5 minutes. Leave to infuse, then strain when ready to use.

Toss the artichokes in the flour, dip into the egg, then roll in sesame seeds. They can be prepared a few hours in advance up to this point – chill, covered, in the fridge until needed. Pour the oil into an oven-proof dish large enough to take the artichokes in a single layer. Add the artichokes and coat in the oil. Roast at 200C/400F/Gas 6 for 30–40 minutes, turning and basting occasionally, until browned.

BAMIA

In this Middle Eastern recipe the okra are simmered in a mildly sweet sour sauce, then left to cool and soak up some of the juice. You can add 250 g (8 oz) or so of peeled, roughly chopped tomato to vary the recipe.

SERVES 4 as a side-dish

½ kg (1 lb) okra, trimmed
1 small onion, chopped
1½ tablespoons olive oil
1 tablespoon caster sugar
juice of 1 lemon

1 sprig of oregano
salt and pepper
1 tablespoon fresh parsley, chopped

Soften the onion in the oil, without browning, then add the okra.
Fry gently for 4 minutes, then add all the remaining ingredients
except the parsley, and enough water to fill the pan to a depth of
about 1 cm (½ in). Stir, then cover and simmer until the okra are
really tender.

Arrange in a serving dish, and serve either warm or at room
temperature, scattered with the parsley.

MUSHROOM AND AUBERGINE MOUSSAKA
WITH GREMOLATA

A no-meat moussaka, but just as filling and delicious as the standard kind. I forgo the usual step of frying the aubergine, which
can make the dish terribly greasy. They cook quite happily in the
heat of the oven.

The final touch, a sprinkling of *gremolata*, the Italian mixture of
very finely chopped parsley, lemon and garlic, gives the moussaka a
zip of freshness to balance the mellow flavour of the slowly cooked
vegetables.

SERVES 6–8 as a main course

1 kg (2 lb) aubergines, thinly sliced
salt
2 large onions, chopped
2 cloves of garlic, chopped
2 tablespoons olive oil

½ kg (1 lb) mushrooms, chopped
½ teaspoon ground cinnamon
1 × 400 g (14 oz) tin chopped tomatoes
1 tablespoon tomato paste
½ teaspoon sugar
pepper ·

Béchamel:

2 tablespoons olive oil
60 g (2 oz) plain flour
500 ml (¾ pt) milk
30 g (1 oz) grated Parmesan or Cheddar
salt and pepper

Topping:

2–3 tablespoons fresh parsley, very finely chopped
zest of 2 lemons, finely grated
1 clove of garlic, very finely chopped
2 large red peppers, grilled and skinned (optional)

Sprinkle the aubergine slices with a little salt and set aside for 30 minutes while you make the sauces. Rinse and pat dry with kitchen paper or a clean tea-towel. Fry the onion and garlic gently in the olive oil in a large frying pan until tender. Add the mushrooms and cinnamon and cook for a further 3 minutes. Pour in the tomatoes and paste, the sugar, salt and pepper. Simmer until fairly thick, for about 10–15 minutes.

While it is simmering, make the béchamel. Heat the oil gently in a medium saucepan and stir in the flour. Cook for 1 minute, remove from the heat and gradually blend in the milk to make a white sauce. Simmer gently for 10 minutes, then stir in the cheese, salt and pepper. Line a greased 25 cm (10 in) square baking dish with the aubergine and season well. Spoon over half the mushroom sauce, cover with a layer of aubergine, salt and pepper. Repeat these layers. Pour the béchamel over the top layer of aubergine. Bake at 180C/350F/Gas 4 for 1 hour, until the aubergine is tender.

Meanwhile, mix the parsley, lemon zest and garlic to make the *gremolata*. Dice the red peppers. When the moussaka is cooked, sprinkle the parsley and lemon evenly over the surface, and dot with the red pepper. Return to the oven for 5 minutes (but no more), and serve immediately.

ONION TART

As a big treat when I was a child, my parents would sometimes take me to the tiny bistro downstairs at La Sorbonne restaurant in Oxford, where they made the most exquisite creamy onion tartlets. This is the nearest I've got so far to recreating them. It's not quite right yet, but I'm getting hot. Had I not been spoilt by their version, I would now be quite content with this.

In fact, I have suggested that you make one large tart – it makes life slightly simpler, although you will find that the filling will ooze out as you cut it. You could, of course, add a couple of eggs to the filling and bake the filled tart until just setting, but personally I prefer it oozing.

SERVES 6
250 g (8 oz) shortcrust pastry

Filling:
½ kg (1 lb) onions, thinly sliced

2 tablespoons olive oil
1 tablespoon flour
150 ml (¼ pt) milk
150 ml (5 fl oz) double cream
salt and pepper
ground nutmeg
60 g (2 oz) grated Parmesan

Line a 23 cm (9 in) tart tin with the pastry. Leave in a cool place to relax for 30 minutes. Bake blind, returning to the oven for 10–15 minutes until lightly browned and crisp.

In a covered pan, sweat the onions very slowly in half the olive oil until soft, stirring occasionally. Make a white sauce by gently heating the remaining oil in a medium saucepan, stirring in the flour. Cook for 1 minute, remove from the heat and gradually blend in the milk and cream. Leave to simmer for 5–10 minutes until thick. Season with salt, pepper and nutmeg. Stir in 45 g (1½ oz) of the Parmesan. Taste and adjust the seasoning.

Reheat the tart case if necessary. Mix the onions with the sauce and pour into the case. Sprinkle with the remaining Parmesan, and brown quickly under a hot grill.

HOT POTATO AND PEPPER SALAD

Waxy-textured salad potatoes don't collapse when cooked and, like new potatoes, are good hot, boiled or steamed.

They are perfect, too, for making potato salads. If you cannot find any proper salad potatoes, use new potatoes. This is one of my favourite potato salads, wildly garlicky.

¾ kg (1½ lb) waxy potatoes
2 tablespoons dried sweet peppers
2–3 cloves of garlic
1 tablespoon red wine vinegar
1 teaspoon French mustard
¼ teaspoon sugar
4 tablespoons olive oil

Boil the potatoes with the dried peppers. Drain, and slice thickly. Peel them now, if you wish to. Peel and crush the garlic and mix with the potatoes and peppers.

While the potatoes are cooking, place the vinegar in a screw-top jar with the mustard, sugar, salt and pepper and olive oil. Close and shake well. Add enough of this vinaigrette to the hot potatoes to moisten well, and serve it hot or cold.

RAW TOMATO SAUCE

This is a favourite summer sauce, marvellous when made with fully flavoured sun-ripened tomatoes. It can be served with hot and cold foods – lovely with grilled meats or tossed into hot pasta. Double the quantity of lemon juice or vinegar and oil, and it can also be used as a dressing for pasta or lentil salads.

SERVES 4–6

½ kg (1 lb) tomatoes, skinned, seeded and finely chopped
1 small, sweet red or white onion, or 2 shallots, skinned
  and finely chopped

2 tablespoons olive oil
1 tablespoon lemon juice, or balsamic or sherry vinegar
1 large clove of garlic, very finely chopped
6 basil leaves, torn up, or 1 tablespoon fresh marjoram,
    chopped
salt and pepper

Mix all the ingredients, cover and chill for 20 minutes. Taste and add more oil or lemon juice if needed, and adjust the seasoning. If necessary, add a pinch of sugar to bring out the flavour.

Main Courses

PASTA WITH ANCHOVY SAUCE AND POACHED EGGS

For years I accepted, sadly, that I was never going to master the art of poaching eggs. I tried this way and that, but it never really worked. After a year of full-time food writing, I decided that this state of affairs couldn't go on. How could I call myself a food writer if I couldn't even poach an egg?

Armed with a dozen eggs, a dozen pans and about as many basic cookery books, I set to. I intended to try out all the tricks that promise perfection, but first I would go absolutely by the book with the most basic method of all. It worked, perfectly. I suspect that my earlier catalogue of disasters may have been due to trying too many of those tricks at a time, and far too nervously.

Two tips for those of you still struggling. The fresher the egg the better the white holds together to give a nice, plump cushion surrounding the yolk. Use the widest non-stick frying pan you can find, then at least you don't run the risk of your eggs sticking to the bottom.

To celebrate my new-found skill, I ate my poached eggs on a bed of pasta laced with a rich anchovy sauce. Wow, was I pleased with myself that evening!

SERVES 2

250 g (8 oz) green tagliatelle
30 g (1 oz) butter
8 anchovy fillets, chopped

4 tablespoons double cream
pepper
2 eggs

Bring a large pan of water to the boil. If your pasta is dried, throw it in before you start making the sauce so that it has plenty of time to cook. If it is fresh, add it once you've got the sauce going. Cook the pasta until *al dente*, and drain well.

Meanwhile, melt the butter in a small frying pan and add the anchovies. Fry gently, mashing the fillets into the butter until they have dissolved. Lower the heat and stir in the cream and pepper to taste. Leave this over a very gentle heat until needed.

Poach the eggs, drain well and trim off any ragged edges. Toss the hot cooked pasta with the anchovy sauce. Pile on to a serving dish and nestle the eggs on top. Serve immediately.

AMERICAN CRABCAKES

I've seen these crabcakes labelled as Baltimore crabcakes, Southern crabcakes, Maryland crabcakes and just plain old crabcakes. The recipes differ only in details, but the theory and essential flavourings remain much the same, and you end up with the most delicious, crisp on the outside, melting inside, all-American crab patties.

Crab is expensive and this is one of the best ways I know of stretching a relatively small amount – roughly the weight you will get out of one medium-sized crab – heartily around 4 people. Mind you, one recipe I found started out with an impressive 2½ kg (5 lb) crab meat and was, it suggested, only enough to feed 10! Now, I would be the first to admit that I could, if hungry and with little else on offer, chomp my way cheerily through two of these crabcakes, but more than that would floor me completely.

SERVES 4

250 g (8 oz) fresh crab meat, brown and white
salt and pepper
1 egg
1 tablespoon mayonnaise
2 teaspoons Dijon mustard
1 tablespoon parsley, finely chopped
4 spring onions, finely chopped
60–90 g (2–3 oz) dried breadcrumbs
oil

Place the crab in a bowl with salt and pepper. Add the remaining ingredients, except the crumbs and oil. Mix, then add enough crumbs to bind. Quarter the mixture, and pat each part into a flat round cake, about 2 cm (¾ in) thick.

Either fry the cakes in a little oil until browned on both sides, or brush the grill rack and crab cakes with oil and grill until well browned on both sides, turning once. Serve with lemon wedges and a green or tomato salad.

RED MULLET AND RED PEPPER TART

Whenever I see it, I find red mullet hard to resist. For a start, it looks so pretty and inviting, with its shiny red skin, and then I know that it tastes pretty inviting too. It has a strong individual flavour, which has given it the reputation of being the 'game bird' of the sea.

It's good grilled and baked (leave the liver in – a delicacy), and has a natural affinity with tomato and fennel. In this recipe I've made it part of a tomato and red pepper tart, flavoured with a little Pernod to give a hint of the aniseed flavour of fennel.

SERVES 4 – 6

250 g (8 oz) shortcrust pastry
2 small or 1 medium red mullet, filleted
8 black olives
extra olive oil

Filling:

1 tablespoon olive oil
1 onion, chopped
1 red pepper, seeded and chopped
½ kg (1 lb) tomatoes, skinned, seeded and roughly
  chopped
1½ tablespoons Pernod
½ teaspoon sugar
dash of red wine vinegar
salt and pepper

Cook the onion and red pepper in the olive oil until soft, without browning. Add all the remaining filling ingredients plus 4 tablespoons of water, or fish stock, and simmer until the sauce is thick. Liquidize, and adjust the seasoning.

Line a 23 cm (9 in) flan tin with the pastry and rest it for 30 minutes in the fridge. Bake the pastry blind.

Cut the mullet fillets into thick strips. Stone the olives and halve. Spread the tomato and pepper purée out on the base of the tart, then arrange the mullet on top like the spokes of a wheel or in a lattice, skin side up, pressing it into the purée. Dot the olives in the gaps. Brush the fish and olives with a little extra olive oil, and bake at 190C/375F/Gas 5 for 10–15 minutes, until the mullet is cooked through and the tart is hot. Serve hot, or warm.

MOROCCAN PAPRIKA CHICKEN

This is an aromatic way of cooking chicken, with rich red buttery juices. Serve it with rice, or better still couscous, to sop them up.

SERVES 4

4 chicken joints
90 g (3 oz) butter
1 medium onion, chopped
1 teaspoon black peppercorns, crushed
2 teaspoons paprika
1 teaspoon cumin seeds
5 cm (2 in) piece of cinnamon stick
1 tablespoon fresh coriander leaves or parsley, finely
    chopped
juice of ½ a lemon
salt

Brown the chicken joints in 30 g (1 oz) of the butter. Remove the chicken from the pan, and gently fry the onion in the remaining fat.

Replace the chicken in the pan, with the peppercorns, paprika, cumin seeds, cinnamon stick and remaining butter. Add enough water to cover. Simmer covered for 1 hour, until the flesh comes away easily from the bones. Take out the chicken pieces, and keep warm. Boil the liquid hard, until reduced by half. Strain, then stir in the coriander leaves, lemon juice and salt to taste. Pour over the chicken, and serve with rice or couscous.

CHICKEN WITH SOY SAUCE

This recipe is rich with dark soy sauce, ginger and sesame oil. Serve with rice or thin Chinese thread noodles to soak up all the sauce.

SERVES 4

1 chicken, or 4 chicken joints
7 tablespoons dry sherry
8½ cm (3 in) piece of ginger
1½ tablespoons cornflour
2 tablespoons oil
4 spring onions, chopped
4 tablespoons dark soy sauce
2 tablespoons sugar
1 teaspoon sesame oil
salt and pepper

Cut the chicken into 8 pieces. Place in a bowl with 3 tablespoons of the sherry. Set aside a 1 cm (½ in) piece of ginger, and slice the rest. Using a garlic press, squeeze the juice out of the sliced ginger on to the chicken. Turn to coat well, then sprinkle with the cornflour. Again, turn and mix so that each piece is covered. Leave to marinate for 30 minutes.

Peel and finely chop the remaining ginger. Heat 2 tablespoons of oil, and brown the chicken in this. Remove the chicken from the pan, and add the ginger and spring onions. Cook over a medium heat for about 1 minute. Return the chicken to the pan, with the remaining sherry, dark soy sauce, sugar, sesame oil, salt and pepper and 5 tablespoons of water. Cover the pan, and simmer gently for 15 minutes, or until the chicken is cooked.

CHICKEN AND TARRAGON PATTIES

These are wonderful, though I say so myself. Crisp on the outside, and then inside creamy, soft chicken scented with just a hint of lemon and tarragon, and the mild sharpness of fromage frais.

Children will love them – at least the ones I had to hand did – but grown-ups may refuse to let them get anywhere near. Serve for a family supper, or a smarter dinner party – they'll slot perfectly into either.

SERVES 4 – 6

125 g (4 oz) fresh breadcrumbs
milk
500 g (1 lb) chicken flesh (use breasts or joints, boned)
1 egg yolk
finely grated zest and juice of ½ lemon
½ tablespoon fresh tarragon, finely chopped
salt and pepper
3 tablespoons fromage frais
1 teaspoon cornflour

Coating:
1 egg, beaten

33

60 g (2 oz) dry breadcrumbs (white or brown)
melted butter or olive oil

Pour enough milk over the breadcrumbs to cover. Mince or process the chicken flesh. If need be, chop it as finely as you can by hand. Place in a bowl. Squeeze as much milk as you can out of the breadcrumbs and add to the chicken with the egg yolk, lemon zest, 1 tablespoon of the lemon juice, tarragon, salt and pepper. Blend the cornflour into the fromage frais, and add this too. Mix well to form a very thick paste.

Chill for 20–30 minutes, or whip into the freeze compartment for 5 minutes, to give the mixture a chance to firm up. Form 8 hamburger-shaped patties, 2–3 cm (1 in) thick, from the mixture (dampen your hands first to prevent sticking). Dip into the beaten egg and then coat well with the breadcrumbs. Leave in the fridge until ready to cook.

Either fry until golden brown in a mixture of butter and oil, or drizzle over a little oil or butter, and grill until nicely browned.

SAVOY CABBAGE AND HAM AU GRATIN

Like many of the best cabbage dishes, this is simple, homely and pleasing. Use the best cooked ham that you can get. If it must come out of a packet, look for one which states clearly 'no added water' – some ham may have as much as 15% or even 20% water pumped into it.

SERVES 2

½ small Savoy cabbage, shredded
salt

125 g (4 oz) cooked ham, cut into thin strips
30 g (1 oz) butter
½ small onion, chopped
30 g (1 oz) flour
300 ml (½ pt) milk
3 tablespoons Parmesan, freshly grated
ground nutmeg
salt and pepper

Drop the cabbage into a pan of lightly salted boiling water. Bring back to the boil and simmer for 1 minute. Drain quickly and run under the cold tap.

Melt the butter and add the onion. Cook until soft without browning, then add the flour. Cook for 1 minute, and draw off the heat. Add the milk gradually to make a white sauce. Return to the heat and bring back to the boil. Simmer gently for 10 minutes, stirring occasionally. Add the cabbage, ham, half the Parmesan, nutmeg, salt and pepper to taste. Heat through thoroughly. Spread out in a gratin dish and sprinkle with the remaining Parmesan. Whip under a very hot grill until the top is nicely speckled with brown.

PORK CHOPS WITH ONION AND
PEAR MARMELADE

Onion *marmelades* and chutneys have shown their faces on countless restaurant menus in the past few years – many of the culinary *maîtres* have taken great and justifiable pride in their perfect, elegant balancing of sweet and sour, onion and spices. To make my *marmelade*, I've added dried pears, which go well with pork, as do most dried fruits. The chutney can be made 2 or 3 days in advance and kept, covered, in the fridge.

SERVES 4

3 medium onions, sliced
60 g (2 oz) butter
175 g (6 oz) dried pears
1 teaspoon coriander seeds, lightly crushed
2 tablespoons white wine vinegar or sherry vinegar
4 tablespoons orange juice
4 tablespoons water
½ teaspoon salt
1 teaspoon dark muscovado sugar
4 pork chops
pepper

Melt the butter, and add the onions. Cover and stew over a low heat for 15 minutes. Slice the dried pears thinly, and add to the onions with the coriander seeds. Stew for a further 15 minutes, then add the vinegar, orange juice, sugar, water and salt. Uncover and simmer until the liquid has evaporated and the *marmelade* is thick and melting. Set aside until almost ready to eat.

Brush the pork chops with a little oil, and sprinkle with pepper. Grill under a well-heated grill until nicely browned and cooked through. Meanwhile, reheat the onion and pear *marmelade* very gently. Stir in any juices exuded by the chops, and serve a good dollop alongside each grilled pork chop.

PORK MEDALLIONS WITH MUSHROOMS AND SORREL SAUCE

Speedy but smart, this recipe. With its generous slosh of cream in the sauce, it isn't an everyday sort of a recipe, but it is a treat worth waiting for once in a while. It's a good number to have up your sleeve for last-minute dinner parties, as long as you can find the sorrel (occasionally available in smarter greengrocers' shops) or grow it yourself. It gives the dish a sharp, green acidity that balances out the richness.

If sorrel is completely unobtainable, use soured cream, and make a mental note to grow your own sorrel next year. It's the one plant I've managed to grow with no problems whatsoever in window boxes, in containers and in the garden. It survives my far from green fingers, so I reckon just about anyone can get it to grow.

SERVES 2 – 3

1 pork fillet
30 g (1 oz) butter
125 g (4 oz) mushrooms, sliced
a handful of sorrel leaves, shredded
6 tablespoons double cream
salt and pepper

Cut the fillet into slices 2–3 cm (1 in) thick. Melt the butter in a frying pan just large enough to take all the fillets. When it is gently foaming, add the meat and fry gently until nicely browned and cooked right through – check one with a sharp knife.

Remove the meat from the pan, and keep warm. Fry the mushrooms in the butter until tender, and arrange around the pork. 37

Add the sorrel to the pan, and stir until it collapses into a purée. Pour in the cream and bring to the boil. Season, and pour over the meat and mushrooms.

SPICED LAMB SAUSAGES WITH TZATZIKI

I do like contrasts of really hot and really cold foods, both temperature- and spice-wise. This combination is hot and cold in both senses, with chillis in one half and cool cucumber and yoghurt in the other.

If you don't have a processor or mincer, buy the lamb and pork fat from a friendly butcher, and ask him to mince them together for you. If you buy lamb on the bone, get a good ¾ kg (1½ lb) meat to allow for waste.

SERVES 4

½ cucumber
1 tablespoon white wine vinegar
salt and pepper
generous 150 g (5 oz) thick Greek yoghurt
1 clove of garlic, crushed
1 tablespoon fresh mint, chopped
500 g (1 lb) boneless lamb (leg or shoulder)
125 g (4 oz) pork fat
1–2 green chillis, seeded and finely chopped
½ tablespoon fresh ginger, grated
½ teaspoon ground cumin
olive oil

38 Dice the cucumber and spread out in a colander. Sprinkle with

the vinegar and a little salt. Leave to drain for 1 hour, then pat dry with kitchen paper or a clean tea-towel. Mix into the yoghurt with the garlic and mint, and season with pepper and more salt if necessary. Chill.

Mince the lamb and pork fat together. Mix well with the chilli, ginger and cumin and a little salt. Break off a small piece and fry to test the seasoning – adjust accordingly. Divide the mixture into 8 and flatten each piece to form an elongated patty about 1 cm (½ in) thick.

Brush the grill rack with oil to prevent sticking. Brush the surface of the lamb 'sausages' with oil too, and grill under a high heat until nicely browned on both sides. Serve with the chilled yoghurt and cucumber.

Puddings

HUNZA APRICOTS WITH YOGHURT

Most wholefood shops stock hunza apricots, although they are easy to overlook. They look drab but they taste exquisite, chewed raw like a caramel or poached with no need for any added sugar. Their caramel richness is quite unlike the taste of ordinary apricots.

They are grown in a remote part of Pakistan, dried on tin roofs in the hills, then transported down the Korkoram highway to be distributed to the rest of the world.

SERVES 4 – 6

250 g (8 oz) hunza apricots
1 tablespoon lemon juice
225 g (8 oz) tub Greek strained yoghurt

Place the apricots and lemon juice in a pan, and add enough water to cover. Bring slowly to the boil, and simmer gently for 5 – 10 minutes, until the apricots are tender.

Once the apricots are cooked lift them out, leaving behind as much of the liquid as possible. Boil hard until reduced by one third, then pour over the apricots. They can be served hot or cold as they are, with a swirl of Greek yoghurt or, if you have the time and the inclination, slit each apricot and extract the stone. Crack this and inside you will find an almondy kernel. Mix the kernels with the apricots.

CRÈME NORMANDE

This is a wickedly smooth, creamy baked custard layered over apples soaked in Calvados. It's so rich that this quantity should be quite enough for 6 people after an ample meal, but I'm sure you'll find that 4 less replete diners will have no trouble getting through it on their own.

Instead of baking it in this way, you could make it the filling for a fruit tart. Line a tart tin with shortcrust pastry and bake blind. At the same time, bake the apples in a single layer in the oven. Spoon into the pastry case and continue as if using an unlined dish.

SERVES 4 – 6

½ kg (1 lb) eating apples, such as Cox's Orange Pippins
4 tablespoons Calvados or brandy
6 tablespoons caster sugar
30 g (1 oz) butter
3 egg yolks
300 ml (10 fl oz) whipping cream
2 tablespoons flaked almonds

Peel and core the apples. Chop roughly and toss in the Calvados. Set aside for 1 hour.

Drain off the Calvados and reserve. Either divide the apple pieces between several small oven-proof ramekins, or put them all into a single oven-proof dish. Dot with butter, and sprinkle with half the sugar. Bake at 200C/400F/Gas 6 for 20 minutes. Beat the reserved Calvados with the remaining sugar, the egg yolks and the cream. Take the apples out of the oven, and pour this mixture

44

over them. Scatter the flaked almonds over the top. Stand in a roasting tray, filled to a depth of 2–3 cm (1 in) with water, and return to the oven. Bake for a further 20–30 minutes until the cream is setting but not yet solid. Serve hot or warm, or cold.

BLOOD ORANGES IN ROSEMARY SYRUP

Why is it that the big supermarkets have started rechristening blood oranges 'ruby red oranges'? It infuriates me. I imagine that the powers that be have decided that the wimpish British public can no longer cope with the proper name. They've been called blood oranges ever since I can remember, and for a long time before that, and a perfectly apt and descriptive name it is, too.

When you get good blood oranges, their juice is an intense dark red with an astringent taste. A glass of that first thing in the morning gets the day going with a tremendous kick. It's delicious, too, relaxed with sparkling mineral water, or a slug of gin or vodka.

My mother laces sliced blood oranges with a gingery syrup to make a light spring pudding. This is a variation on her theme, born out of necessity – no ginger in the house, but facing me on the spice shelf were 2 jars, dried rosemary and Szechuan peppercorns (delicatessens and oriental supermarkets). It's a stunning marriage of flavours. The syrup seems strong at first, but is diluted by the juice of the oranges.

Out of season, use ordinary oranges. Black or green peppercorns can be substituted for the Szechuan peppercorns. Serve it on its own, or with a chocolatey pudding, such as a mousse, for grander occasions.

1 teaspoon Szechuan peppercorns, or green or black
  peppercorns
150 g (5 oz) caster sugar
150 ml (¼ pt) water
1 sprig of rosemary
6 blood oranges or 4 large oranges

If you use Szechuan peppercorns, dry fry in a small heavy frying pan over a high heat, until they begin to scent the air with incense. Put the sugar, water and rosemary in a pan. Coarsely crush the peppercorns of whatever sort and add those too. Stir over a medium heat until the sugar has completely dissolved. Bring to the boil, turn down the heat, and simmer for 5 minutes. Cool until tepid and strain.

Pare the orange zest off 1½ small oranges, or 1 larger one, and shred. Drop into a small pan of boiling water and blanch for 1 minute. Drain, and dry on kitchen paper. Peel all the oranges, removing as much of the bitter white pith as you can, and slice thinly. Place in a bowl, and pour over the syrup. Scatter with shredded zest. Leave in the fridge for at least 1 hour, and serve lightly chilled, with crisp biscuits.

NEW YORK CHEESECAKE

The New York cheesecake is the best of them all, I was told firmly when I visited the city. Uncluttered and unfussed, creamy and light, with a hint of lemon and a hint of vanilla.

46   They have got a point. So here we are: a recipe for the ultimate

baked cheesecake, not cloying and gluey, as they are far too often, but a dream of simplicity.

SERVES 8

Base:

250 g (8 oz) graham crackers, if you can get them, or digestive biscuits
90 g (3 oz) butter, melted

Filling:

500 g (1 lb) cream cheese
½ teaspoon vanilla essence
juice and finely grated zest of 1 lemon
3 eggs, separated
125 g (4 oz) caster sugar
2 tablespoons cornflour
150 ml (5 fl oz) soured cream

Pound the biscuits to crumbs in a plastic bag or processor. Mix thoroughly with the butter. Press evenly into the base of a greased 23 cm (9 in) springform cake tin. Chill while you make the filling.

Beat the cream cheese with the vanilla, lemon juice and zest until smooth. Add the egg yolks, then 60 g (2 oz) of castor sugar, cornflour and soured cream and beat until well mixed. Whisk the egg whites until stiff, add the remaining sugar, and whisk again until smooth and shiny. Fold into the cream-cheese mixture.

Spoon on to the biscuit crust, and smooth over the surface. Bake for 55–60 minutes at 170C/325F/Gas 3, until nicely browned. The filling nearest the outside should feel firm to the touch, though the very centre will still be slightly gooey – it will 47 continue to cook as it cools. Leave to cool, then run a thin knife blade around the edge, and ease the cheesecake carefully out of the tin. Chill for 4–12 hours in the fridge before serving.

BLACKBERRIES IN FILO PASTRY

This is a simple way of transforming dull farmed blackberries, bringing out a flavour that's close to that of wild blackberries. Of course, it's even better made with blackberries brought back from a ramble in the countryside. *Crème de mûres* is a blackberry liqueur. Look out for miniatures in well-stocked wine shops, or use the more widely available *crème de cassis*.

SERVES 6

90 g (3 oz) cream cheese
1 tablespoon crème de mûres *or* cassis
125–175 g (4–6 oz) blackberries
60 g (2 oz) sugar
2 sheets filo pastry
30 g (1 oz) butter, melted

Sauce:

250 g (8 oz) blackberries
2 tablespoons crème de mûres *or* cassis
extra sugar if necessary

Make the sauce first: pick over the blackberries, removing any that are damaged. Place in a pan with the liqueur. Heat gently until they begin to exude juice, then simmer for 5 minutes. Remove from the heat, and sieve or pass through the fine blade of the *mouli-légumes*. Taste, and add sugar if necessary, though the sauce should be slightly tart.

For the filo parcels, beat the cream cheese with the *cassis*. Mix the blackberries with the sugar. Halve the sheets of filo pastry lengthways, and divide each strip into 3 squares. Take 2 squares, brush with melted butter and lay one on top of the other. Place a heaped teaspoon of the cream cheese in the centre and top with blackberries. Gather the pastry up and around, twisting the ends together to form a money bag. Sit on a buttered baking sheet. Repeat until all the ingredients are used. Brush the bags with any remaining butter, cover and set aside. They can be made up to 3 hours in advance.

Heat the oven to 250C/475F/Gas 9. Bake the filo bags for 7–10 minutes, until browned. Divide the sauce between 6 individual plates (reheat it if you like – I prefer it cold). Sit a hot pastry in the centre of each plate and serve, with single cream if desired.

FROZEN CHOCOLATE MOCHA MOUSSE

This is the most superb pudding, simultaneously an ice-cream and a mousse, rising majestically above the rim of its bowl in imitation of a hot soufflé.

Use the best plain chocolate you can find, with a high percentage of cocoa solids. Be careful not to overheat the chocolate when melting – it loses its gloss and turns grainy. Remove from the heat the very moment it has melted.

SERVES 8

250 g (8 oz) plain chocolate, broken into squares

1 tablespoon high-quality instant coffee
4 eggs, separated
125 g (4 oz) sugar
300 ml (10 fl oz) whipping cream
icing sugar

First prepare the mould. You will need a 14–15 cm (5½–6 in) soufflé dish. Cut a strip of greaseproof paper or foil 15 cm (6 in) wide and long enough to go round the dish, the ends overlapping by 2 cm (1 in). Wrap around the dish, leaving at least 5 cm (2 in) sticking up above the rim, and secure with sticky tape. For extra security, stretch an elastic band or tie a piece of string around the dish just below the rim. Brush the inside of the paper with a little tasteless oil.

Melt the chocolate with the coffee and 2 tablespoons water, and cool slightly. Whisk the egg yolks with the sugar, until thick and pale. Mix with the melted chocolate. Whip the cream until soft peaks form. Fold into the chocolate. Whisk the egg whites until stiff, then fold in too. Spoon into the prepared mould, and smooth down gently. Freeze.

Move from the freezer to the fridge 10–15 minutes before serving. Carefully remove the paper collar and dust with icing sugar just before taking to the table.

CRANBERRY TART

There's more to cranberries than sauce, and turkey, and Thanksgiving or Christmas dinners, nice though all of those are. The cranberry is an odd fruit, when you think about it. That characteristic bitter astringency makes them quite unlike any other, begging for some kind of softening sweetness, even when they are to be transformed into a sauce for meat.

As winter approaches, and punnets of cranberries crowd on to the greengrocers' shelves, I begin to use them in abundance. This buttery translucent tart exploits their unique flavour well.

SERVES 6–8

Pastry:

125 g (4 oz) plain flour
125 g (4 oz) wholemeal flour
125 g (4 oz) butter
1 tablespoon oil
1 egg, beaten
salt

Filling:

250 g (8 oz) cranberries
250 g (8 oz) caster sugar
125 g (4 oz) lightly salted butter
2 eggs
30 g (1 oz) flaked almonds

Sift the flours with the salt. Rub the butter into the flour. Make a well in the middle and pour in the egg and oil. Mix with enough cold water (this may be as little as one tablespoon) to form a dough. Set aside in a cool place for 30 minutes to relax.

Place the cranberries in a pan, with 2 tablespoons water and 60 g (2 oz) sugar. Heat gently, stirring, until the sugar has dissolved and the juices begin to run. Bring to the boil, and boil rapidly until the cranberries have all burst – 5–8 minutes. Off the heat, stir in the remaining sugar and the butter. Leave to cool.

Line a 25 cm (10 in) tart tin with pastry, prick the base with a fork, and rest again in the fridge for 30 minutes. Heat the oven to 190C/375F/Gas 5 and bake blind. Whisk the eggs into the cranberry mixture, and pour into the pastry case. Scatter with the almonds, and bake for 30 minutes. The filling will puff up slightly as it cooks – but once out of the heat of the oven it will soon settle. This tart can be served hot, but is best just warm with a dollop of whipped cream.

MARMALADE ICE–CREAM WITH WALNUT SAUCE

Being a schoolgirl in Oxford brought many benefits. I'm not sure that my friends and I really appreciated the heady intellectual atmosphere of the colleges, but we took full advantage of many of the extra-curricular pastimes spawned by the University. The summer months were particularly pleasant – punting and boating, Shakespeare plays in beautiful college gardens, watching cricket in the Parks, or the Eights races on the Isis. And, of course, there were the students themselves.

A curious shop came into its own in May and June, at least as far as I was concerned. In a side street off Cornmarket, one of Oxford's main streets, was a cramped bookshop. As well as books, it sold wrapping paper and cards, and the most inventive range of homemade ice-creams. The choice changed weekly. There were usually all the basics – vanilla, chocolate, strawberry, and so on – but there was always at least one 'joker'. The two that have stayed most in my mind are the witty smartie ice-cream and, best of all, their marmalade ice-cream. The slight bitterness of Seville oranges

on the tongue, rich and creamy. I think the shop has now dis-
appeared, but the memories linger on.

For preference, use homemade marmalade for this ice-cream –
if you make your own, it's a good way to clear the shelves, before
the winter's new arrivals. Otherwise, try to buy a jar of 'extra-jam'
marmalade, with a high proportion of fruit to sugar.

SERVES AT LEAST 8

Ice-cream:

375 g (12 oz) marmalade
300 ml (10 fl oz) double cream

Sauce:

4 tablespoons marmalade
150 ml (¼ pt) orange juice
150 ml (¼ pt) water
sugar to taste if necessary
45 g (1½ oz) walnuts

To make the ice-cream, tip the marmalade into a large bowl and
beat. Whip the cream until stiff, then fold into the marmalade.
Freeze. This is one of those miracle ice-creams that doesn't need
beating as it freezes, and can be served straight from the freezer
– a marvellous thing, that double cream.

For the sauce, place the marmalade, orange juice and water in
a pan, and simmer together for 10 minutes. Taste and add sugar
if necessary. If you are feeling very conscientious (and it will
improve the taste), remove the clinging papery skin from the
walnuts as follows: cover with boiling water and leave for
30 seconds. Drain, and peel. Be patient.

If you aren't feeling so conscientious, just break the walnuts into small pieces and, off the heat, add to the sauce. Serve the sauce hot or cold, with the ice-cream.

ISABEL ALLENDE · *Voices in My Ear*

NICHOLSON BAKER · *Playing Trombone*

LINDSEY BAREHAM · *The Little Book of Big Soups*

KAREN BLIXEN · *From the Ngong Hills*

DIRK BOGARDE · *Coming of Age*

ANTHONY BURGESS · *Childhood*

ANGELA CARTER · *Lizzie Borden*

CARLOS CASTANEDA · *The Sorcerer's Ring of Power*

ELIZABETH DAVID · *Peperonata and Other Italian Dishes*

RICHARD DAWKINS · *The Pocket Watchmaker*

GERALD DURRELL · *The Pageant of Fireflies*

RICHARD ELLMANN · *The Trial of Oscar Wilde*

EPICURUS · *Letter on Happiness*

MARIANNE FAITHFULL · *Year One*

KEITH FLOYD · *Hot and Spicy Floyd*

ALEXANDER FRATER · *Where the Dawn Comes Up Like Thunder*

ESTHER FREUD · *Meeting Bilal*

JOHN KENNETH GALBRAITH · *The Culture of Contentment*

ROB GRANT AND DOUG NAYLOR · *Scenes from the Dwarf*

ROBERT GRAVES · *The Gods of Olympus*

JANE GRIGSON · *Puddings*

SOPHIE GRIGSON · *From Sophie's Table*

KATHARINE HEPBURN · *Little Me*

SUSAN HILL · *The Badness Within Him*

ALAN HOLLINGHURST · *Adventures Underground*

BARRY HUMPHRIES · *Less is More Please*

HOWARD JACOBSON · *Expulsion from Paradise*

P. D. JAMES · *The Girl Who Loved Graveyards*

STEPHEN KING · *Umney's Last Case*

LAO TZU · *Tao Te Ching*

DAVID LEAVITT · *Chips Is Here*

PENGUIN 60s

LAURIE LEE · *To War in Spain*

PATRICK LEIGH FERMOR · *Loose as the Wind*

ELMORE LEONARD · *Trouble at Rindo's Station*

DAVID LODGE · *Surprised by Summer*

BERNARD MAC LAVERTY · *The Miraculous Candidate*

SHENA MACKAY · *Cloud-Cuckoo-Land*

NORMAN MAILER · *The Dressing Room*

PETER MAYLE · *Postcards from Summer*

JAN MORRIS · *Scenes from Havian Life*

BLAKE MORRISON · *Camp Cuba*

VLADIMIR NABOKOV · *Now Remember*

REDMOND O'HANLON · *A River in Borneo*

STEVEN PINKER · *Thinking in Tongues*

CRAIG RAINE · *Private View*

CLAUDIA RODEN · *Ful Medames and Other Vegetarian Dishes*

HELGE RUBINSTEIN · *Chocolate Parfait*

SIMON SCHAMA · *The Taking of the Bastille*

WILL SELF · *The Rock of Crack As Big As the Ritz*

MARK SHAND · *Elephant Tales*

NIGEL SLATER · *30-Minute Suppers*

RICK STEIN · *Fresh from the Sea*

LYTTON STRACHEY · *Florence Nightingale*

PAUL THEROUX · *Slow Trains to Simla*

COLIN THUBRON · *Samarkand*

MARK TULLY · *Beyond Purdah*

LAURENS VAN DER POST · *Merry Christmas, Mr Lawrence*

MARGARET VISSER · *More than Meets the Eye*

GAVIN YOUNG · *Something of Samoa*

and

Thirty Obituaries from Wisden · SELECTED BY MATTHEW ENGEL